Stolen From Africa

KOKUMO ROCKS

Luath Press Limited
EDINBURGH
www.luath.co.uk

First published 2007
Reprinted 2009
Reprinted 2016

ISBN: 978-1-906307-19-6

The paper used in this book is recyclable. It is made from low-chlorine pulps produced in a low-energy, low-emission manner from renewable forests.

The publishers acknowledge the support of

 Scottish Arts Council

towards the publication of this volume.

Printed and bound by
Harper Collins/RR Donelley, Glasgow

Typeset in 11 point Sabon
by 3btype.com

© Kokumo Rocks 2007

KOKUMO ROCKS was born in Dundee, but was raised in the Fife mining village of Cowdenbeath. Hers was the only black family in the area, and she left school with no qualifications and an inability to spell. It wasn't until she attended university in the late 80s that she was diagnosed as dyslexic.

In 1991 she decided to change the direction of her life following a near-death experience, and began to fulfill her life-long dream to become a performance poet. Since then, she has published two books and spoken to countless individuals about the appreciation of poetry through her poetry workshops for adults and children. She developed Scotland's first Black History course at a community school (Leith Academy), and recently launched Scotland's first school poetry library (Crichton Primary). For the last four years she has been teaching a writing course for people from disadvantaged areas, and continues to inspire people to appreciate poetry and put an end to racism through her performances. She took part in Kofi Annan's Global Peace Initiative in Geneva, and went with a small delegation to Israel/Palestine.

Her media appearances have included speaking on BBC Radio Scotland about the Abolition of the Slave Trade. She is a participant in audio conferences on conflict resolution in the Middle East, and performs in Storytelling events through the National Library of Scotland.

In spring 2007 Kokumo took part in a poetry reading/play entitled Human Traffik about black Scottish slaves who worked towards Abolition. She was the black history consultant for the Scottish Churches Racial Justice Annual Conference, which took place on 16 June 2007 to mark the Bicentenary of the Abolition of the Slave Trade in Scotland. She also gave a speech at the conference on the role of female black Abolitionists in Scotland and the US.

Her future plans include completing a PhD in Black History, and working on a book about Scotland's role in Black History.

She describes herself as an African/Asian/Scottish writer and performance poet, and has performed in the UK, USA, Canada, India and Africa.

Kokumo – the name means 'this one will not die' – lives by the motto 'if you don't ask you won't get', and believes that 'passion can turn the mundane into excitement'.

I dedicate this book, in the year of the Bicentenary of the Abolition of the Slave Trade (1807–2007), to the 50 million noble African men, women and children slaves who died in horrific circumstances for the greed of others.

For my sons Jason and Darren, friends and supporters, I love and appreciate you all. Many thanks for being in my life. I hope you will stay for a long to come, xxxx.

A special word to Rose Clark, who has been in my life since my teens; I love having you in my life. You're the best friend any woman could possibly have! You are humanity and compassion at its best, xxxx.
PS: *Jason and Darren love you too!*

My hope: 'May humanity and compassion return to our world soon!'

Contents

Foreword	ix
Introduction	xi
Let's Hear It For The Orange	1
Given A White Leg	2
Stolen From Africa	3
You Didn't Invite Me	4
Love Is Greener Than War	5
Seductive Wind	6
I Loved You	7
Disarmed and Derobed	8
Boundless Freedom	9
Jeans Cut Off At The Knees	10
Belong Where?	11
Becoming Terrorists	12
The Bully	14
Megalomaniac Butterfly	15
Tartan Earmuffs	16
Barbie and Ken	17
Snow Dance	18
Cruel Snow	19
Flames	20
Change	21
Sonnet (Not) For 'She' The Boxer	22
A Bronze For Life Saving	23
Viva Nigeria	24
Refugees Welcome Here (Not)	25
War, What Is It Good For?	26
Taking Off Unearthed	27
Dying Delightfuls	28
The Jersey	29
A Spectacle	30
Hair Today, Gone Tomorrow	31

When Time Stood Still and Fell Asleep	32
It's My Chair	33
The Truth Is Out There	35
7 MSPS In One Blow	36
ID Cards No Thanks	37
Nobody To Blame But Us	38
Kaz's Secret, Aged 13½	39
Coffee Shop Secret	40
Haiku	41
2 4 6 8 2	42
The Van Ran	43
The Edge	44
Passion For Life	45
High In Rio	47
Two Girls	48
See You See Me	49
Always On The Bus, Never On The Street	50
The Ghost Grave	51
Dam	52
Sonnet To A Gull	53
Belly Itch	54
Crawlies Up Your Nose	55
Gypsies, Not In My Backyard	56
Darfur Why For	57
My Name Is Number 4	58
Yellow Orb	60
Keep The Candle Alight	61
Hey Brother	62
Tom 5	63
Shell Shocked	64
The Cowdenbeath Black Panther Movement Fae Fife	65
Red Horse	67
In The Attic	68
Fleeting Moments Of Pleasure	69
Autumn Snaffodils	70

Foreword

GOETHE, IN HIS Conversations with Eckermann, is reported to have said of poetry, 'What need of much definition? Lively feeling of situations, and power to express them, make the poet.'

Kokumo Rocks' second book is confident and aware, looking less to an audience and more to the inner truth of herself and of the poems. Kokumo is a brilliant performer and many of the poems are for performance but this does not mean they are not also thoughtfully written poems for the page.

Kokumo has an extraordinary talent for taking up some everyday object or happening and transforming it into a vehicle for argument, delight, ridicule or sheer joy, eg., 'the jersey, cross-stitched... weaving stories and lives lived'; the Snaffodils 'ready to bloom from the darkness of decay'; the spectacles 'facing downwards' and 'observing upwards'.

Then again Kokumo can bring tears to the eye in the simplest lines of imaginative compassion: 'In the attic/ I left you the moon'; 'the truth is out there... but we hurry past' and 'Will our children bury their children?'

Kokumo's mixed heritage is unique and she makes it the more so by beautifully celebrating it and making Scotland the richer for it. Her poem about the amputee demanding a black leg is hilarious but also politically and sociologically profound, as is the poem about the child in a wheelchair who feels trapped by being 'always on the bus, never on the street.'

Kokumo takes trouble with her poems, finding the right word, the best rhythm and style for each poem. She frees us from our thraldom to words while at the same time setting words free in the service of her art as poet, performer, activist and historian.

Tessa Ransford

Introduction

I LIKE MY POEMS to be edgy, humourous, sensual, passionate – with a political bite.

I write to share my loves and concerns because I think there is an urgency to protect our world and cherish our citizens. To share power, not bask in it. To enjoy the gifts of the earth and keep our hopes and dreams alive and embrace all, and retain our sense of fun in the face of life's trials and joys.

This book is the next step in a lifetime's journey. To climb to the top of the mountain and try to view the world with different eyes, fresh perspectives. As a writer to catch the moment, dive into the ocean, to find a pearl, sifting sands, waiting apprehensively for a bite. Losing consciousness, finding an alternate one. Fishing for inspirations, a word, an idea, a verb, food for the soul, like smooth nectar drizzling down the throat. Smiling as the ideas grow, groaning as they depart, disappear, dissipate. Tomorrow, start over, mark the blank page, and wrestle with creativity, discipline and the lack thereof. A juicy process not for the fainthearted.

Still, inspirational writers run round my brain like Maya Angelou, Jackie Kay, Ivor Cutler, Ben Okri, and Anita Desai, as well as new writers I've heard, and wonderful, poignant work written by refugees and asylum seekers in Glasgow, Edinburgh and London.

I grab ideas from the world around, the sky, rain, sassy seagulls, jealous lawnmowers, Barbie and Ken rolling down hills, and the freedom to roam in the mountains and glens of Scotland.

I write for my life, your life, the animals and the trees, but I'm still trying to understand Sudoku, technology and geometry.

Kokumo Rocks
Edinburgh
November 2007

Let's Hear It For The Orange

Let's hear it for the orange
Tangy juicy in yer face poser
Strutting amongst the trees
When ripe, it falls waiting
To be picked up
By Lords I presume

When opened it gives out
A zesty zing
A friendly smack in the face
Stating 'life's tough so
Jist get oan whey it'
And enjoy
Let's hear it for the orange

Given A White Leg

'Can I have a black leg?'
'Oh, here's your white leg madam and good luck'
'Sorry, didn't you hear me?
I said I need a black leg'
'Sorry madam, they don't come in black'
'What do you mean they don't come in black?'
'There's not much call for black legs in London'
'Good grief woman, don't you know how many black people
 live here? Your hospital runs on the backs of blacks'
'Sorry madam, that's not my department.
If madam insists she needs a black leg it will cost you £2000'
'£2000?'
'Yes madam, plus VAT'
'Plus VAT?'
'Yes, madam needs to calm herself down.
I have given you a leg, now you have two legs to stand on,
So be calm'
'Calm? I'll give you calm, you supercilious prat'
'Come now madam, there's no need for such behaviour'

Excuse me! My behaviour!
Please! Just take your white leg
And melt it!

And I'll see your boss in court
Good day!

Stolen From Africa

15 million died, the rest flogged
To the highest bidder
But the slaves soon ran
Revolted from Haiti to
The Scottish lands
Black men like Wedderburn
And Spens
United all to fight
Till they were freed
From 1807–1833
15 million spirits of the dead
Joined in and sang
In one united breath
Free at last
Free at last
Thank God Almighty we're
Free at last

You Didn't Invite Me

One day a gang of yellow combs
Were having a steak barbeque
On the new mown lawn
Followed by a glass of beaujolais
And a few root beers
When a disgruntled lawnmower
Trundled over and gobbled them all up
Spitting out their yellow teeth
Bellowing
You didn't invite me suckers

Love Is Greener Than War

Love is greener than war
War is like a pomegranate, blood red
Dribbling then clotting as it trails out of a wound
A wound larger than Leningrad
A pulsating time bomb of destruction
The human capacity to forget their compassion
Which slopes off down the dark October road
Leaves crushed into the ground
Watery sun gone down
The barren earth reflects the despondency
Created
Bodies thrashing about, riddled with sharpened bullets
That cut into the heart
The screams echoing the thoughts
We've gone too far this time
As the solitary figure steps out from the edge of darkness
Scraping up the knarled gristle that was once a
Gurgling child
These screams stay held in the night
The walls telling silent tales of horrific scenes
Gone past
Will the stones crumble soon and reveal all?
Will the night let go its secrets?
Will our children bury their children?
Or will love creep back stealthily from under the
Shadow of death to embrace us all
Till we grow full and remember

Seductive Wind

Seductive carefree wind
Playing with my mind
Ruffling my hair
You sweep in caressing my body
With your relentless embrace
My curtains billow
You've crept under the door
Singing dangerous songs
Of longing
Fixing me with your steely gaze
Your icy grip leaves imprints
Your gusty advance
Is like being dragged
Into a vortex
With no escape
But you slow down
Becoming gentle
Warming
I breathe in the silence
And lie still
Relaxed

I Loved You

I loved you with an open heart
Where violins played and daisies danced
Now I love you still
But your heart is closed
And the violin strings are broken

Disarmed and Derobed

Disarmed and derobed

I plunge into a field
Drinking in its nectar
Dancing in time to the
Swaying flowers
Letting the juice drip
Onto my tongue
Tickled I sing louder
Clearer
Caught in the intensity of love

Boundless Freedom

Doors without locks
Locks without keys
Landscape
No walls nor windows
Paths leading nowhere
I dream lost in a haze
Wandering along
The stony trail
Copper flecks glint (in the sun)
Beads of sweat trickling down
Water bottle uncapped
Mouth drools in anticipation
Liquid cool as crushed ice
Lips parted ready to embrace
The rushing torrent
Ah! Smack!

Jeans Cut Off At The Knees

Today I glanced in the mirror
And a stranger looked back
Saggy lids, rheumy eyed
Behind them
Laughs a rebellious teen
Jeans cut off at the knees
pierced belly-button
Flaps in the wind
Tattoos telling of the world
Muscles and sinews parade passion
About the universe
What to eat, who to save
Causes to support
Brand of coffee to drink
Whose friends to have sex with
Whom to fall out with and in again
At night she laughs with pleasure
Swimming in the ocean with naked abandonment

Belong Where

Mixed race
Mixed face
Mixed hair
Mixed roots
Mixed up
Belong here
Belong where
Nowhere!
Scream!

Becoming Terrorists

Hey you, I didnae hear ye ask
Tae speak oan oor behalf
Youse lot nivver dae
Ye come tae speak
Rant at demos
But youse wurnae invited
No cause yiv nothin' tae say
But 'cause yir no listenin'
Seein' hearin' ever
Hey! Over here
I'm the wan wavin'
Wi the red tammy oan
Nae luck invisible
Youse jist keep spoutin'
An' bletherin' sh*te
Poorin' watter 'til
Wur droned, exasperated
Kin ye no hear the din
Of the tortured screams
Wur scunnered bein' talked tae death
So shut yer gob
An' hear us
Youse lot are turnin' us intae terrorists
Cause wiv hud enough
Oor brains are oan fire
Wiv lost oor desires
Wur shaken in oor shoes

Wiv hud too much booze
Thurs somethin' in oor haunds
Wir pointin' it straight at you
Enough!

The Bully

The bully's comin'
The bully's comin'
Run run run
O'er the fence
Shaken, oot o' breath
Grabbing Jamie, 3
Jist in time

Oh hell
The bully's comin' back
Run run scatter
Flippin' heck Jamie's fallen
He's bawlin'
The bully's nearly
Oan tap o' him
Jamie staunds up
Pokes out his tongue
Wiggles his bum
Grins

The bully lifts his haunds
Jamie starts to dance
Then prance
We creep oot
And staund a'hind him
The bully half grins
Smirks and skulks away
Yes! Saved for another day

Megalomaniac Butterfly

One day a megalomaniac
Butterfly

With period cramps
Landed on a caterpillar grub
Seeds of recognition
Shook her to the core
She stomped, yelped
Threw a hissy fit
Screeching I could
Never have been
That bug ugly
Or was I?

Tartan Earmuffs

Dear Aunty

Thanks for the prezy
Tartan earmuffs in summer
What a wondrous idea
Useful to keep the flies
At bay
To dull the drone of bees
And naff summer songs

Like tack adoo doodooo
Put pineapple in your shoes
Squelch to the left
Then give yourself a fright

Barbie and Ken

One day a fairy princess
Sprinkled silver dust on Barbie and Ken
Immediately on waking they started bitching
Ken accused Barbie of having an affair
Barbie said Ken was lame and wet
Still it all ended in tears of joy
As Barbie went off with Cindy
And Ken fell in love with himself

Snow Dance

Luscious snow
Flakes unfurling
Fragile and intricately formed
Like a Monet
Sculptured, fine-tuned
As a perfect note
The flakes dance
Floating down
In slow time
Creating a carpet
On which to lie
But not to rest

Cruel Snow

The snow hurled itself downwards
Like a malevolent essence
Shape shifting everything it touched
'Til all the world became it
All corners blurred
Density seemed shallow and insane
The world appeared to crumble at a touch
Colours disappeared
Everything stopped
Journeys aborted
Machines seized up
Pipes burst
Windows cracked
And fish froze

Flames

The flame bobbed and weaved
Like a boxer
As the wind skipped
By lamenting on
Extinction

Change

Change, does it hurt?
What does it look like?
What does it feel like?
What is it?
Why is it?
What's it for?
Can we buy it?
Throw it away?
Eat it?
Sleep with it?
Dunk it in tea?
Take it for a walk?
No! Stop!
Stop thinking, asking
Just change it
Whatever that is?
Argh!

Sonnet (Not) For 'She' The Boxer

What are you thinking woman of fight?
Whose every move he does contest
You maketh this man afraid take flight
His survival becomes an unholy test
You weave and scamper very well
Yon punch does make him rock and reel
This man is grateful for the bell
He can be treated for what he feels
The final round is yet to come
Bruised and battered your opponent fell
Victory points to the final sum
The end is nigh he craves the bell
Yon man does rest and not return
The best woman in the fight has duly won

A Bronze for Life Saving

I saved my life the other day

But I nearly threw it away

Down the river into the gutter
Without a mutter from me
Quietly disappearing without regret
Just letting it slip away
A precious life
Full of ardour, Tupperware
And glee
The scent of grass
A baby's soft arse
And nectar filtering
Down from the trees

Viva Nigeria

I wrote for the first time in June
The urge came surging like the river Niger
I wrote scalding hot prose
For a city named Lagos
The metaphors were as succulent
As the flesh of papaya
As the words raced down the page
Like a sea of humans
In Yabba Market
The sentiments rippled across my mind
Like lovers between silk sheets
In Ipaga
Their emotions smouldering
Like the setting sun
On Africa's red earth
While I awake
With love for her elegance and grace

Refugees Welcome Here (Not)

Innocent refugees fleeing war
Met with derision and suspicion
Incarcerated, locked up, tied down
Shackled by policies based on greed
Demonised, dehumanised
Their children cry, scream to get out
To roam along freedom street
To crawl through the door
Play hide and seek with friends
Not men with keys and guns
So scared they cannot eat or sleep
Terror of being sent back by men in suits
Finally suicide

War, What Is It Good For?

War, what is it good for?
Absolutely nothing, say it again

War, what is it good for?
Absolutely nothing, say it again

Scream no to legitimised murder
Say no to desecrating lives
Stop the massacres
Shut down our leaders
Shake up those in charge
Before it's too late
Before it's too late

Open the gate to communication
Open the gate to all in unison
Open the gate to peaceful living
And sing the world to rights

War, what is it good for?
Absolutely nothing, say it again.

War, what is it good for?
Absolutely nothing, say it again

Taking Off Unearthed

The blades burled
The engine revved
My eardrums vibrated
Like a drill
My brain ricocheted
Round the inside
Of my skull
While a blast of air
Sent my hair skywards
I was unearthed

Dying Delightfuls

The sun and the day deceased
In glorious rays of colour
While the trees shook
And the leaves felt a chill
Whispering, 'Autumn has come again'
'Nearly time to die,' they sang cheerfully
'Let's go out in a blaze of reds and honey golds'
They hired artistic ants
And golden thread spiders
Task done, they animals flocked to gape
At the luscious canopy
As the end grew nearer
The leaves started to shiver and fall
Floating down gracefully
In a twirling dance
Laying out a brilliant carpet of colours

The Jersey

The jersey, cross-stitched
Moved in time with the wearer
Weaving stories and lives lived

A Spectacle

The spectacles lay on the table
Legs awry, lenses facing downwards
Observing upwards

Hair Today, Gone Tomorrow

I have an internal grow bag
Inside my skull
That needs no feeding but continues to sprout
Maybe it's the magic fairies
Or the effervescent elves
Weaving golden threads of recollection
Curling around, keeping intact silver memories
Aiding visionary glimpses
From deep inside
That could dissolve in a flash
Though shadows may hang around
For you to grasp
If you talk sweetly to those fairy elves

When Time Stood Still and Fell Asleep

Rocks to be climbed
Mountains to assail
Worlds and words to conquer
Striding without sound
Silence impacting on my ear
Talking to my boots
I continue upwards
Rolling rocks trundle by
Murmuring stories of disturbance
Unsettled by vibrations
Invisible hand
Stillness sidles in
Stopping time
Time leans lazily on the hill
Having forty-winks

It's My Chair

It's my chair. Yes
The power is all mine
To sit and rule, rule you
You obey because the rules are inside,
Inside your head
Confused, I think so
'Cause I did it
Don't waste your time
Trying to equalise yourself with me
I have the chair
Though I did not build it
I sit here and dream in my power
Stroke my chair
And kiss its ass
Like you do mine
It's my chair
I vamp on it, tramp on it
You come to make peace
Peace breaks my hold
Evaporates my gold
I want to be you, have you
Having you would wreck my goals
I won't give in, you won't win
It's my chair, my power
It cradles me like a comfortable throne
You treat me like a king
You talk about me with awe

Foolish fools
Look behind you
You are me
I have absolute power
It's my chair, it's my chair

(Inspired by the play 'Where's the Power' by The Elements)

The Truth Is Out There

The truth is out there
So I believe
It hides in corners
Sleeps in boxes
Shouts out occasionally
I'm over here!
No, over here!
But we hurry past
iPod on high
Pulling sweets off shelves
Strolling into a pint of beer
Blanking out
As the truth slips quietly by
As the truth slips quietly by

7 MSPs In One Blow

I've never seen seven green
Forests or fields with legs and brains
Committed to saving the earth's dreams
Talking and walking
The grassroots' needs
Pushing the boundaries of
Establishment's graves
Growing monuments
To fresh views and
Earthy ways

ID Cards No Thanks

Work passes bus passes breathing passes
Train passes farting passes
And now ID cards

Computer codes post codes funeral codes
No sex on Wednesday codes
And now ID cards

ASBO laws no smoking laws
Criminalise the poor laws
No pension till your 90
Shoot to kill laws
And now ID cards

DNA checks fingerprint checks
Hairy armpit checks passport eye checks
Bum cheek checks
And now ID cards
No thanks
Not in my name

Nobody To Blame But Us

Nobody to blame but us
Nobody to blame but us

We blew out the sun
Nobody to blame but us

All the fish choked on oil
Nobody to blame but us

We strangled the crops and poisoned
The land
Nobody to blame but us

We obliterated the tigers and the bears
Nobody to blame but us

Then we annihilated everyone
Nobody to blame but us

Then we blew up our world with
Nuclear bombs

Nobody to blame but us
R.I.P.

Kaz's Secret, Age 13½

Feeling sad
Cutting arms
Feel bad
Do some more
Blood on the floor
Nobody knows
Kaz's secret

Coffee Shop Secret

You came by
Skin pierced by silver
Inky cloak shrouding you
In secrets
Your face spoke of a myriad of continents
Bearing questions – who are you?
What are you?
Why?
Your plaits snake out from
Beneath your hat
Slithering down your velvet cloak
You turn, stare, signal to leave
But the questions remain unanswered
Who are you?
What are you?
Why?

Haiku

The café lit up
Beckoning in dark shadows
Silhouettes go dance

The fat cow nodded
Listening well as the pig
Swilled out stupigness

The song ran uphill
Coughing and spluttering tunes
Running out of notes

The broom swept swiftly
Hurrying along the dust
Which tore up a storm

2 4 6 8 2

Lanterns
Outside mischief
Dresses ultimately
To be evil incarnately
Gruesome

Sit down
Be quiet now
Get your books out today
Hurry or you will be sorry
My lads

The Van Ran

The van slid into the gravelled drive
Its brakes screeched
Like a demented hog
The gravel uprooted
Clattered, splattered along the path
Smashing into the newly glazed door
Breaking through, onto the wooden floor
With a dainty crash

The Edge

Over the table edge
Lay the blank paper
Snared by the chair
Going nowhere
Rippling in the breeze
Calling the writer
To start

Passion For Life

I run like an animal exhilarated
Wind rushing past my bum and the space
Between my thighs
As I stride out pounding the earth
Stamping on the world
I inhale life catching my own breath
I run faster, feeling the phoenix rising
From my gut
As arched back four legs gallopping
I fly over stones, rivers and bones
I climb, soar, body extending
No longer human
I tear through the earth
The caverns light up as I pass
Rivers incase me
The wind rides on my back and
The sun hides from my brilliance
I converse with the gods
And Zeus joins in for a run
Together like feathers we glide then
Dive under mountains flying out
The other side
We gather in rain clouds
To slake our thirst
Which burst, creating oceans
Where whales leap and seahorses prance
And we keep on entranced, enhanced

Ablaze with passion for life
For life
Ablaze with passion for life
For life

High In Rio

High in Rio in a samba trance

Flying off Yesu's head
Sliding onto the 'Bonde' tram

While dangling off the tracks

Shifting down to
Coco cabaña's sands
Swerving to the Flavellas streets
To dance the night astray
Swaying home in the wee
Sma' hours
Set to play the
Next day

Two Girls

Two girls
Same eyes
Same skin
Same hair
Same love
Mirrors
Mirrored
Reflections
Looking black
Talking black
Together

See You See Me

See you see me
See you see me
Say what's your game?

Cause I'm fed up telling you and spelling you my name
Telling you where I'm from, where I'm really from
Who's my Dad and what's the biggest smoke I ever had

See you see me
See you see me

Is it an inability or a disability
To see past your face that Britain is made up of many a race
We're not being quiet and we will cause a riot
Till you see us and hear us on an
Equal basis

See you see me
See you see me

Always On The Bus, Never On The Street

Always on the bus, never on the street
Stuck in my wheelchair
Collected from home
Dispatched at school, wheeled inside
Bussed home again

Glaring through the glass
As people walk past
Feeling the rain on their faces
The rain it pours down the drain
With a sook
Two boys run, jump, splash
Into a puddle
I gaze at the magic in their eyes
As they laugh and run off
I sigh and my bus departs

To bed I dream, I'm lying on the grass
Sun beating down, warm on my skin
Outside is fun watching the birds
Sh*t on the grass
The daisies whisper hello
James we're glad you're off the bus
I laugh and the wind ruffles my hair
And I feel happy again

The Ghost Grave

Where is she?
Searching in vain
Where is she? We gasp
Undergrowth flattening
Beneath our feet
Craning our necks
Kicking over rubble and stones
Throats threatening
Desperate sounds
Eyes bearing liquid
We crash on
Feet determined
Shoulders set
Not giving in
Not giving up
Ever
We'll find you
Find you soon
And flowers will be
Strewn in your name
And flowers will be
Strewn in your name!

Dam

I will not be decieved this time
I will not be decieved this time

You lied about Malcolm
You killed Martin
You are a nation of well-meaning racial hypocrites
The worst kind
Kindly ignoring, shuffling and looking away
Waiting to see if others will do, but not you
Eat your croissants and sip your ale
And discuss anything that's looking pale
Not dangerous
Disturbing your quiet dream
Your stroll in the park
Your peaches and cream

But don't scream if the alienated, dissaffected
Ride by shooting at you
Killing your dog
Don't scream to the Paki, the immigrant, the black
To save your ass
Cause the rivers of blood are flowing
To your door and I don't want to talk to you anymore
I don't want to hear what you have to say
I'm not interested in your salvation
Your responsible for your own damnation

Sonnet To A Gull

The gull does come to peck my nose
I think I shall this try to stop
'Cause he has also grabbed my clothes
Alas his end has dropped a plop
Onto my hair which he has soiled
I recoil in disgust and fear
Oh drat that gull my hair is spoiled
The filthy rat pooed in my ears
I tried to clean and wipe it off
But green and messy it becomes
As this mad gull just laughs and scoffs
Ignores the fact this makes him scum
Now I shall never be at peace
As damned seagull my hair is grease.

Belly Itch

Hello my favourite ant
You crawl and scurry
Making my belly itch
Now you drop to the floor
Hurry through the door
Goodbye my dear ant
Let no one crush you
Underfoot
Splat!

Crawlies Up Yer Nose

On a sunny day I happily
Fall through the earth
Below the soil

Creeping crawlies slither
Up my nose
Entering all orifices
I squirm, shudder and scratch
Wondering why
I felt inclined to fall
Beneath the earth

On such a sunny
Day

Gypsies, Not In My Backyard

I'm invisible, a hub cap
A radiator, a noise
When I brake, stop
I become a live myth in your head
A liar, a thief, a smell
Animated you organise
So we can return
From whence we came
But we have a secret
To tell as we roll along
The wind is always at our backs
The earth bears fruit as we pass
A thousand stories come from our lips
As we breathe in the sky
And shoot out the stars
While a bucket catches the rain
Our children sleep soundly
Drinking in the knowledge of the earth
As we stroll along
In peace

Darfur Why For

Sudan, Sudan, here we go again
Government reactive, never proactive
More than enough to go around
But the government's will goes underground
Drowning in their own greed
Their emaciated spirits dying
From lack of trying
If the government's generosity
Was a sustainable crop
The lack would create world famine
Ministers' bellies swollen from stewing
In their own inept juices
Their eyes sucked in from too many
Late feasts
Always sickening for more
Too fat to stoop to the floor
For food
Nobody hears their cries
As they screech why oh why
Sudan screams back the same
As five thousand die
Why for God's sake, why?
Oil!

My Name Is Number 4

My name is number 4, number 4
I know this because it's drawn inside
My welly boot
In ink!
It's free time and I'm sitting on the floor
Cause there's no chairs
Or anything more
I've swallowed my porridge
And tried to leave
The lumps
But it's been forced down my throat
By an enormous hand
Numbers 22 and 26 are doing the dishes
And 10, my friend, is locked up
So I have to play alone

I stare at the chimney pots, smokey brown
The gates won't open for another hour
Then we'll have free assembly
Outside in half an hour
If the work is done right, very right

Laundry cleaned, yard swept
Floors polished
Lined up for inspection
Rags in hand
As a huge index finger
Slides slowly along a ledge
Looking for dust and finds some
So the gates stay shut
No free time today
And numbers 33 and 7 are to take
The blame again
My name is number 4, I know this
Cause it's drawn inside my welly boots
Written on all my name tabs in ink!
Oh happy days!

Yellow Orb

Yellow orb radiating
Like a god
Soothing our hasty world
Which slows down
As you melt our hearts
Covering them in love
Exuding warmth from your blood

Keep The Candle Alight

She kept the candle alight for me
Cherishing, cradling, crooning it awake
As I slept
Slipped in and out of sorrows
She bathed my soul in love
Washing out sad stories
As she breathed in light
Resuscitating my heart
Wrapping it in a pink blanket
Crying away my tears
As she gently nestles me against her warm bosom
I felt my strength return, revived
Slowly opening my eyes
I planted a kiss on her cheek
In thanks

Hey Brother

Hey brother you came from the street
That's pretty neat
But you've not got my face
You're a different race
Hey brother
Hey brother
You wanna be Scottish and claim this land
But the streets in the US are a different land
The poverty, killing and isolation
Is the same for the youth in this tartan nation
Hey brother
Hey brother
Racists exist and homophobic nits
No jobs, no hope, and plenty of dope
Hey brother
Hey brother
So speak your own mind
And don't rap the isms
Of the moneyed kind
Hey brother
Hey brother

Tom 5

A slight boy
With warts on his chin
Unable to sit still
So locked in his room
Shouts, 'Hey mirror
I'm a dead good boy
I am
Tomorrow
Everyone will notice
When I get it right
Please God!'

Shell Shocked

Explosions erupting, deep hole in the ground
Scattered debris, echo of a bang
People stumbling shocked
Somewhere a silent scream escapes
As a boy slips past drenched in blood
The quiet hush breaks
Emotions explode, erupt
Leaving a deep hole in the communal psyche

The Cowdenbeath Black Panther Movement Fae Fife

Yo brothers and sisters
Salutations from the Cowdenbeath
Black Panthers Fae Fife

Yo we're here
To state our demands
In this bloodless coup
Aims self government
For yoofs
We decide the rules

Objectives: A better life
Like real jobs
And having fun

Requirements: Hot trainers
Cool music
Black shell suits embossed
Legalised Iron Bru
Rapid fire water pistols
Ten Darth Vadar masks
Tons of deep fried Mars bars

And the voices heard
Of the black rural yoofs
ok ya baz

Salutations from the
Cowdenbeath Black Panthers
Fae Fife

'Whatever'

Red Horse

One day a red horse
Sat in a field having tea and toast
When a flying fish
Fell from the sky
And banged him
On the nose

In The Attic

In the attic
I left you the moon
Knowing it would
Light up your life
Let you drink in its magic
Bathe in its brilliance
Believing it would
Cherish your soul
Caress your heart
Telling you love stories
From afar

Fleeting Moments Of Pleasure

Fleeting moments of pleasure
Are rarely captured by a book
But drawn into the memory
Like the glance
Of a blinking eye
To live forever
Or slowly fade and die

Autumn Snaffodils

The snaffodils' sunny disposition
Declines
As the petals curl turning brown
Leaves dropping down
The once erect stem
Moaning as the head droops
Leaning hard
Almost touching on its own roots
The golden haze fading fast
Leafage crumbling before the eye
But there is a seed left below
Ready to bloom from the darkness of decay

PS 'So that's alright then'

Some other books published by LUATH PRESS

Bad Ass Raindrop
Kokumo Rocks
ISBN 1 84282 018 4   PBK £6.99

- What would happen if a raindrop took acid?
- Does your bum shake and does your belly wobble?
- And have you noticed that there are no black babies on 'New Baby' cards?

Fadeke Kokumo Rocks' first collection of poetry is alive with love, passion, humour and brutal honesty. It is sharply observed, potent and insightful, capturing beautifully the sixth dimension of the creative eye. It has a rich diversity of time and content, which embraces the globe and its conflicts, domestic and urban.

You can hear the monsoon rains of Africa, taste the mangoes of India, touch the compassion and spirit of the child and sense the pain of burning flesh as race riots rage.

Read the eclectic, electrifying poetry of Kokumo Rocks in this collection containing over 30 of her most popular poems. Full of Kokumo's distinctive humour, *Bad Ass Raindrop* challenges the questions we answer unquestioning. Kokumo has been performing her poetry for over ten years. Equally entertaining read or performed, Kokumo's distinctive voice and unique brand of humour shine through.

Rocks' work speaks of Africa and India... of racism, injustice and black pride. But she refuses to confine herself to discussions of race. There are waves and beaches, Leith schoolgirls, sex, shopping, Aids and raindrops that take acid.
THE HERALD

... there is a distinct and addictive zest about many of the poems.
THE LIST

Luath Press Limited
committed to publishing well written books worth reading

LUATH PRESS takes its name from Robert Burns, whose little collie Luath (*Gael.*, swift or nimble) tripped up Jean Armour at a wedding and gave him the chance to speak to the woman who was to be his wife and the abiding love of his life. Burns called one of 'The Twa Dogs' Luath after Cuchullin's hunting dog in Ossian's *Fingal*. Luath Press was established in 1981 in the heart of Burns country, and now resides a few steps up the road from Burns' first lodgings on Edinburgh's Royal Mile.

Luath offers you distinctive writing with a hint of unexpected pleasures.

Most bookshops in the UK, the US, Canada, Australia, New Zealand and parts of Europe either carry our books in stock or can order them for you. To order direct from us, please send a £sterling cheque, postal order, international money order or your credit card details (number, address of cardholder and expiry date) to us at the address below. Please add post and packing as follows: UK – £1.00 per delivery address; overseas surface mail – £2.50 per delivery address; overseas airmail – £3.50 for the first book to each delivery address, plus £1.00 for each additional book by airmail to the same address. If your order is a gift, we will happily enclose your card or message at no extra charge.

Luath Press Limited
543/2 Castlehill
The Royal Mile
Edinburgh EH1 2ND
Scotland

Telephone: 0131 225 4326 (24 hours)
email: sales@luath.co.uk
Website: www.luath.co.uk